Developing Children's Liturgy

A Step-by-Step Guide

Gail Fabbro

Resource Publications, Inc.
San Jose, California

Reprint Department
Resource Publications, Inc.
160 E. Virginia Street #290
San Jose, CA 95112-5876
1-408-286-8505 (voice)
1-408-287-8748 (fax)

Library of Congress Cataloging-in-Publication Data
Fabbro, Gail, 1937–
    Developing children's liturgy : a step-by-step guide / Gail Fabbro.
      p.   cm.
    ISBN 0-89390-443-0 (pbk.)
    1. Children's liturgies. [1. Catholic Church—Liturgy.]
    I. Title.
    BX2045.C553F33   1999
    264'.0203'083—dc21   98-55178

Printed in the United States of America

99 00 01 02 03 | 5 4 3 2 1

Editorial director: Nick Wagner
Prepress manager: Elizabeth J. Asborno
Production coordinator: Mike Sagara
Copyeditor: Robin Witkin

Excerpts from the English translation of the General Instruction of the Roman Missal and Directory for Masses with Children from *Documents on the Liturgy* © 1982, International Committee on English in the Liturgy, Inc. All rights reserved.

Excerpt from *Music in Catholic Worship* Copyright © 1983 United States Catholic Conference, Inc., Washington, DC. Used with permission. All rights reserved.

Illustrations by Noelle Deinken
Cover photography by Ralph Swanson

Contents

Introduction

When You Know Absolutely Nothing About Planning Children's Liturgy

This book is a practical guide to planning a liturgy with children. It does not presuppose that you know anything about developing a liturgy. It is a friendly book that will carry you along with ease.

This book is written for all those who pray the liturgy but have never planned the liturgy. It is for those who work with children in the classroom but have never worked with them in the church. This book is for those teachers who have just graduated from college and whose first job is teaching in a Catholic school. It is for those catechists in the religious education program whose experience has never included developing Masses with children. It is for anyone who needs help in the area of children's liturgy.

Begin with the practical and the spiritual will follow. When your class is asked to plan a liturgy and your knowledge of how to do it is minimal, just pray and trust and read this book.

This book is divided into three parts: for beginners (and before), for catechumens (learners), and for the fully initiated, liturgically speaking. The first part is for those who have never, or have rarely, planned or developed a liturgy with children. This part uses a "trust" liturgy planning sheet found in Appendix A. This means that a person who has no knowledge of liturgy planning can take the sheet, trust it completely, and plan a liturgy for children. The ritual will speak and the experience will happen.

Many times we have to learn by doing, which may not be the definitive way to approach liturgy, but it may be all we have in the beginning. Because you have attended no in-service, class, or workshop that guided you along the path of children's liturgy, you can rely on the first planning sheet to carry you through initially.

The second part, for the catechumens, helps you learn all you can about what is going on, and how and why and when. The third part, for the fully initiated, invites mystagogia and gives you the opportunity to continue the work you have begun and to put into practice all that you have learned. Remember, we must form ourselves before we begin to form the children.

Part I

In the Beginning

If this is an emergency—if you are in charge of a liturgy next week for the first time—turn immediately to Liturgy Planning Sheet I in Appendix A and the guidelines on page 7. Follow them and all will be well. If instead, you have a little time to prepare, read the following for a bit of background.

This chapter has no citations, resources, or suggested books. You only have to believe that this is a chapter you can trust. Clear your mind; concentrate on what is on the printed page of the "trust" planning sheet and follow it. You will be surprised at the result. You will have a prayerful liturgical celebration, and you will be calm all through the stages of development and during the celebration itself. What comes out of your mind will affect everyone's heart.

Let's assume your class has been asked to plan a liturgy. Only a few things must be taken care of by you and your class:

- You must choose the readings.

- You must write the prayers of the faithful (also called the general intercessions).

- You must plan the procession to bring up the gifts of bread and wine.

- You must plan for silent prayer after communion.

You might also be asked to choose the music for the liturgy.

If you have a music minister available in your school or program, your first liturgy will be even easier to plan because the only book you will need is the *Lectionary for Masses with Children*. Leave the music selection to the music person.

Before you do anything else, you must decide what readings you will use. Let's assume you know what season the church is in—Advent, Lent, Ordinary Time, Easter Season, and so on. If you do not know, ask someone.

The *Lectionary for Masses with Children* is divided into the seasons listed above. For our purposes we will choose Ordinary Time. We are speaking now of weekday Masses because that is what you will be dealing with primarily. Each set of readings is titled with a suggested focus. You may have run across some planning resources that speak of a "theme" for the liturgy. It is not quite correct to use the term *theme*, because the theme of every liturgy is the life, death, and resurrection of Jesus—the paschal mystery. However, we can focus on different aspects of the paschal mystery in a particular liturgy.

The focus could be for instance, "show faith by actions" or "give thanks to God." Choose a set of readings and then choose your readers. Choose one reader for each reading, but do not try to give everyone in your class a "part." There is a suggested time during the Mass when all the children can be visible and model their prayerful attitude. We'll discuss that later.

Go over the readings with the children. This helps the readers and also familiarizes the other children with the focus of the liturgy. Talk about the readings during one of your religion classes. You choose a particular set of readings because you feel that these are the readings the children should hear proclaimed at this time.

Note that the readings in the *Lectionary for Masses with Children* do not correspond with the adults' *Lectionary for Mass*. The readings in the *Lectionary for Masses with Children* are written for children, and not all of the readings in the adult lectionary are included. You are free to choose any set of readings in the *Lectionary for Masses with Children*.

During the session in which you introduce the readings, you can also begin writing the general intercessions. Depending on the age level of your children, either discuss in general what should be prayed for or write down specific petitions after some discussion. The petition format is included in the planning sheet. It is not necessary in Masses with children to adhere strictly to the format or to include everything. But it is good, at least, to know what the format is and what prayers are usually included. The "For...that" structure—For people who do not have enough to eat, that...— will make the petition simple and clear.

You will need to choose two children to bring up the bread and wine at the gifts procession. Choose only two children and bring only bread and wine to the altar. It is always appropriate to have the altar servers who carry the cross and the candles process down the aisle and lead the people up in the gifts procession. Please note that this part of the Mass is known as the presentation and preparation of the gifts. We have shortened it and will continue to refer to it as the gifts procession.

Have a proper procession with the gifts. Place the bread and wine on a table in the back of the church. There are two ways to get the bread and wine carriers to the back of the church. One way is to have the bearers of the cross and the candles come down from the sanctuary area; as they pass the pew that the carriers are in, the carriers join the procession, go to the back of the church, pick up the bread and wine, and process back up the aisle. Another way is to have the bread and wine people go directly to the back of the church when everyone stands for the general intercessions. After the intercessions, the cross and candles carriers process to the back of the church and lead the people with the gifts to the altar.

You might suggest to your music minister that it would be proper to sing or chant all acclamations. If you start this at the beginning of the school year, it will be automatic by the end of the school year. Your music minister will know what acclamations are to be sung, but for your own planning, you may want to remember that they include the acclamation before the Gospel; the Holy, Holy; the memorial acclamation; and the amen at the end of the eucharistic prayer.

Even though Part I is the "bare bones" part, one additional element can be added with ease. Have the presider call the class "in charge" around the altar for the eucharistic prayer. Have the children walk up slowly to the worship space with their hands folded in front of them, and have them actively participate in the eucharistic prayer. Let the presider choose the prayer he is most comfortable with unless you know that the children are familiar with one of the eucharistic prayers for children. If that is the case, you might want to suggest that prayer to the presider. The children should stand in a semicircle around the altar until after the Our Father. At that time they offer a sign of peace to the person on each side of them and return to their seats in a single or double file.

After communion, plan silence. This is one of the best things you can do and also one of the easiest. Silence leaves a place for the Holy Spirit to enter freely and without interference. Children are very rarely encouraged to sit back and pray in silence. It might be a novelty for them.

Now that you have everything written down on your planning sheet, communicate with the presider. Talk to the priest who will be celebrating the liturgy with you. If he is not available, make sure that the planning sheet is put on his desk, in his mailbox, or wherever he will be sure to see it. That is absolutely essential. There is nothing worse than meeting the presider in the sacristy five minutes before Mass and trying to explain whatever needs explaining and reminding him to take the planning sheet with him so he can remember to call the children around the altar.

The next step is to go over to the church and rehearse the children. At this liturgy they are a model for the rest of the children. Everything should be laid out for the rehearsal just as it would be for Mass. Perhaps there is someone in your school or religious education program who is appointed sacristan for all the Masses. If so, make full use of this person who will set out the sacred vessels, altar cloths, dishes, books, and whatever else is used in the liturgy. Sometimes the altar servers do all this, but it is good to have someone else oversee their work. This is the practical side of liturgy and helps keep everything running smoothly. You should not have to worry about the presider sending one of the servers back to the sacristy to bring out some forgotten item. You should be able to trust completely whoever is in charge of this part of the liturgy.

As you are planning your "trust" liturgies, begin to think of the flow of the liturgy. What should be emphasized? What is primary and what is secondary? Because you are putting your faith in the simple outline of the planning sheet, you can begin to notice the flow and balance of the parts of the Mass. You do not have to concern yourself with "thinking up" every little detail, and you can look on the liturgy as a whole. Step back and let your mind view the liturgy in its entirety. Look at the peaks and valleys and see the flow. Be aware. Full, active, conscious participation boils down to awareness. By using the trust planning sheet, you can see that the Introductory Rite does not overshadow, for instance, the Liturgy of the Word. There is nothing stuffed into the liturgy that might distract the students' minds from what is really going on. The liturgy is not entertainment. It requires as much input from the assembly as from the "people in charge."

For the next two or three liturgies you plan, it might be a good idea to use this simple planning sheet until you are comfortable with the process. This may take all year if your class plans one all-school liturgy and one or two class Masses, but it is worth it. You will be grounded in something that you will be doing as long as you are involved in a school or religious education program.

Now that you have planned, developed, and celebrated your first school liturgy, you will never again be a novice. The liturgy was beautiful because it was simple and you were confident and the children were well rehearsed. The Holy Spirit entered in, as the Holy Spirit always does. We do our work and the Spirit does the Spirit's work. We always leave room for the human and let God take care of the divine. It works well.

Guidelines for Using the Liturgy Planning Sheet 1

Begin at the very beginning.

- Open the *Lectionary for Masses with Children*. Turn to the liturgical season we are presently in. Choose the set of readings you think should be the focus for the liturgy.

- Choose the readers for the first reading and for the general intercessions. (The psalm is always sung or chanted, so your music minister will take care of that.)

- Choose the children who will carry up the gifts, bread and wine only.

- If there are altar servers in your class, choose five of them to participate—two to serve at the altar, two to carry the candles, and one to carry the cross.

- Look to your music minister for musical advice and for help in choosing the songs.

- Go over the readings during your religion class or catechetical session and discuss the general intercessions.

- Rehearse in church with the children in charge. Keep the rehearsal simple.

- Rehearse the entrance procession. Your group is a model for the rest of the children at this liturgy.

- Rehearse the responses with the children and with the altar servers.

- If the presider is going to call the children around the altar during the eucharistic prayer, rehearse that. Let the children go up in single file, ending with a curved line on each side of the altar.

- Rehearse going up to share communion.

- Rehearse the silence after communion. It is good to remember that when you rehearse, that is also praying.

- Be sure to make an appointment to see the presider, or leave a copy of the planning sheet for him well before the liturgy. (Leave a copy for him on Monday if you have a Friday liturgy.)

- The presider will choose all of the presidential prayers (the prayers in the sacramentary). You will not be expected to do this at this time.

- On the day of the liturgy, make sure that there is someone in charge of setting out what is needed for Mass. Will it be the altar servers, the elected school representative, or will it be you? If it is you alone, familiarize yourself with the sacristy and all it contains well beforehand.

Part II

Catechumenate Period

Congratulations! You have planned your first liturgy. Now you can take a little breather until the next time. This interim, "The Time of the Second Planning Sheet," should be calm. You are comfortable with the actual planning of a children's liturgy and can now reach down into deeper thought, the drawing out of the children's life experience. This is the time to study the liturgical documents (*Directory for Masses with Children* especially), familiarize yourself even more with the *Lectionary for Masses with Children* and generally take your time and develop a rhythm of learning and developing liturgy. You are becoming aware of what children's liturgy really is. When your knowledge becomes advanced, you can plan, develop, and experience the faith of the children. Begin to feel the nuances of the liturgical elements. Remember what you have done before in planning liturgy and look to the future. Let your thoughts percolate. Become liturgically aware of what can be included in a Mass with children, how it can be included, and why it should be included.

Probably "why" is the question you must most often ask yourself. Anything included in the liturgy should be there to enhance the participation of those in the assembly. If it does not do that, it should not be included. Ask yourself if what you are putting in the liturgy—skits, gestures, songs, dances—would be better presented in the school auditorium. That is a determination for you to make with your educated judgment. What we take from liturgy is experienced in our lives every day; and we bring our everyday experiences to liturgy. Liturgy is where you pray those experiences; life is where you live them.

The *Directory for Masses with Children* will make more sense to you after you have developed a few liturgies. Reading directions in a foreign language does not help your comprehension until you have lived in that country for a while. While you are looking through the liturgical documents, look as well for classes, workshops, in-services—anything that would have to do with children's liturgy. Attend conferences; sign up for sessions offered in your diocese. Now is your learning time. Now is when you develop confidence in what you are doing. Take advantage of anything that is offered in the way of liturgy with children, but don't confuse it with Liturgy of the Word for Children. That is another category altogether and includes (as is stated) only the Liturgy of the Word, not the entire Mass.

In learning, you will discover something about yourself. You will discover that your own spirituality is deepening, that your understanding of what is going on in life is more acute. This is not knowledge that you impart only to the children—this is your life, too. This is your living, breathing sense of the Three Persons of the Trinity. You do not only "go to Mass"; you participate in all that is happening in liturgy. This is your life that you are developing, too.

The second liturgy planning sheet is probably the one that you will use the most. It delineates all the parts of the Mass, and by the time you are ready to use that sheet, you will be familiar with those parts.

You and your children will usually plan a liturgy for the entire school or the entire religious education program only once a year. However, there are many opportunities for a class Mass or a prayer service in which you would incorporate the Liturgy of the Word, processions, songs, gestures, intercessions, and silence. These could be planned once a month or so, perhaps for a saint's feast day, for a special cause, or simply in thanksgiving. Use both the first and second planning sheets as a basis for your prayer services. Use the second planning sheet as a guide to familiarize yourself with the sacramentary.

In the beginning, the priest will choose all presidential prayers (those he prays). However, there may come a time later on when the presider has not seen your planning sheet—as in the case of a last-minute change of presiders. The presider may then ask you to mark in the sacramentary the prayers that he will be using.

If your school or religious education program does not have easy access to a copy of the *Lectionary for Masses with Children* or to a sacramentary, you must obtain a copy. Most parishes have copies of these books in the sacristy, but that will usually be inconvenient for your purposes. Ask if copies can be kept in the teachers' or catechists' workroom or some other easily accessible place. Part of the reason we do not become familiar with these books is that they are not close at hand. If you have not attended a workshop or in-service on planning children's liturgy, you can create your own "workshop" by reading the introductions to the *Lectionary for Mass* and the *Lectionary for Masses with Children*. Read them several times until you begin to understand what is being said. You will understand the texts even better as you begin to plan and implement liturgies. But how do you start planning a liturgy if you don't know what you are doing? That is why, in the very first place, you must trust. Trust in a competent authority, even though you may have questions that cannot be answered in the time before the liturgy.

Eventually, you must trust yourself. You have read and listened and experienced and, most of all, prayed. You will be fine.

There is much you can do to advance your understanding of liturgy so you can approach it without apprehension. Your parish probably receives a plethora of printed matter, which many be termed *junk mail*. But there is no such thing as junk mail. Take a look at that mail and see what is being offered. You might be surprised at what you may be able to use. Take a little time to scan what has been sent. Every so often you might find a gem of a book or pamphlet that is just what you have been looking for. At certain times of the year, there are also some good buys on materials. It is always worth a look. Ask the secretary to put the mail in a basket that is accessible to you. Go through it when you are waiting for people to gather for a meeting or during other "empty" time.

If we did not have rules and guidelines, someone would have to invent them. Some people disagree. They say that what is important is that we pray. God listens and does not care how we pray. But we are not God, and we need to know what we are doing. We need to express ourselves verbally and visually, and we need ritual in which to do it. That is why we have documents such as the *Directory for Masses with Children* to lead us more deeply into the experience of the paschal mystery. We cannot go off and create our own differing rituals, although sometimes it seems as if that is what we are doing. Liturgy is not entertainment. Liturgy is not show business, and we do not have to tap-dance to hold people's attention. Expunge from your vocabulary the word *creative* when referring to children's liturgy. We do not need to create anything. What we need is already there. But, you say, we must adapt for the children, we must say the words in a way that they will understand, and we must spark their full, active, conscious participation. All that is true, but it has nothing to do with the word *creative*. What we must do is draw out from the children their way of expressing their faith. We don't want to impose our way of thinking about how their faith should be expressed. We want to encourage a real understanding of their lives and their ways of expression. Draw out; never stuff in.

All that we need in liturgy is already there. We just need to learn how to use it. Choose the right songs, proclaim the readings properly, plan processions, gestures, and visuals—but use your poetic eyes and see that those elements are intrinsic in the liturgy and have everything to do with the particular focus. Anything manipulative should never be in liturgy. A "performed" song, readings proclaimed in an inordinately dramatic manner, or anything that is done because it is cute or clever, clearly does not belong in liturgy. If the paschal mystery is not enough, then we had better rethink what we are all about. Save the other activities for the school hall or the classroom.

Here is an example of the point I am making—Santa Claus at the children's Mass on Christmas Eve. If we include Santa in the liturgy—no matter how humble and prayerful he is at the manger—should we not have the Easter Bunny bring up the gifts at Easter? Or perhaps the Tooth Fairy can make an appearance sometime during the year. Why do we pretend that Santa Claus is real by including him in our scriptural Christmas story? Give Santa his due in the classroom. Let him roam the school yard. Or celebrate St. Nicholas Day on December 6. Show the children where the real spirit of Santa Claus came from. Embellishments such as Santa in the liturgy definitely qualify as entertainment and confuse the focus.

Going Through Planning Sheet 2

Entrance Procession and Gathering Song

Processions can be included early on in your liturgical education. After all, the entrance procession is a procession and the gifts procession is a procession. Begin with these and do them well. Depending on the architecture of your church, the entrance procession could take place all around the inside of the church with everyone singing with gusto. The purpose of a gathering song is to "help the assembled people become a worshiping community and to prepare them for listening to God's Word and celebrating the Eucharist (*General Instruction of the Roman Missal* 24). Of these parts the entrance song and the opening prayer are primary. All else is secondary" (*Music in Catholic Worship* 44).

Now you know to choose a song that unifies, that will generate enthusiasm and eagerness to participate. By now you and your music minister have worked out a way to collaborate on the choice of songs and have a repertoire that works. There may be a time when you would begin outside the church and process around the block (if pedestrians and traffic accommodate). Walk around the outside of the church, chanting. Station several people strategically in the procession who can keep up the chant. If you do this in May or October, pray the rosary as you walk. Try a procession during Lent or a joyful anticipation procession during Advent. You can also declare your liturgical focus during the entrance procession. Is your focus baptism, for instance? In that case, perhaps each member of the class can carry up a small container of water from different familiar sources (their own kitchen tap, the lake where they spent their vacation, melted snow, water from the Holy Land, water from Lourdes, water from their favorite watering hole), and when they reach the worship area, mingle it with water already provided in the church. The presider would then bless the water and a sprinkling rite would take the place of the penitential rite.

Perhaps it is the beginning (or the end) of the school year. Those visuals (basketballs, textbooks, globes)—that were always incorrectly included in the gifts procession—can be presented in the entrance procession. Visuals that enhance the environment or direct attention to the thrust of the liturgy are also candidates. Whatever is carried in should need no explanation. Let the symbol speak for itself. Liturgy should never be explained; it is to be experienced.

Regarding visual elements, the *Directory for Masses with Children* has this to say, "In addition to the visual elements that belong to the celebration and to the place of celebration, it is appropriate to introduce other elements that will permit children to perceive visually the wonderful works of God in creation and redemption and thus support their prayer. The liturgy should never appear as something dry and merely intellectual" (35).

Use the songs that the children love. They do not have to be "children's" songs. There are many songs that speak to both children and adults. If the children know these "Sunday" songs, let them sing them during the week, too. Choose songs that the children know well, that they sing as one, that contribute to a joyful celebration.

Penitential Rite/Sprinkling Rite

When the new sacramentary is approved, the section containing the Introductory Rite will most probably offer different choices for that rite. The most significant for children's liturgy would be the separation of the Kyrie from the penitential rite. The Kyrie, which is now included in the penitential rite, will become a litany of praise.

What this means to us now, and to those who adapt the Kyrie for children's liturgies, is that we must make certain that it isn't a recounting of sins ("For the times I wasn't nice to my brother and sister…"). The Kyrie should be what it had always been and is always supposed to be—a litany of praise. The confusion came because this form was included in the penitential rite. You can avoid this confusion by using the invocations printed in the sacramentary. The children will understand them. There are eight invocations. Do not try to adapt them; they are fine just the way they are.

You are also free to choose a sprinkling rite in place of the penitential rite.

Opening Prayer

Take a look in the sacramentary. Even though it may not be up to you to choose the presidential prayers, you should be familiar with one prayer for now—the opening prayer. Take one step at a time, and you will not be overwhelmed. Look at the opening prayer.

On a regular weekday, the presidential prayers to be used are the prayers for the previous Sunday. Therefore, if last Sunday was the Fourteenth Sunday in Ordinary Time, you will use those prayers in the sacramentary all during the week. We will keep it simple for now.

Look only at the opening prayer. Do not take on too much at once. You will see that there are two prayers—a suggested prayer and an alternate one. Read them and choose the one you think would be most appropriate. This is just an exercise in your liturgical instruction. It does not take too long, but it will help a great deal later on.

Liturgy of the Word

Use the *Lectionary for Masses with Children* to help decide which set of readings focus on what you feel should be prayed in the liturgy. Make sure that you are in the correct liturgical season.

Remember that when the readings are proclaimed, they are never announced. Have the children say, "A reading from the letter of ..." rather than "The first reading is a reading from ...." In like manner, the psalm response and the response of the people are chanted or sung, not introduced.

The homilist will need the planning sheet well in advance. You may also have spoken a few words to the priest regarding the emphasis of the readings. There will be times when what you have suggested is not what you hear in the homily—even though your suggestions incorporate what you feel the children should hear. Remember that the Holy Spirit speaks to everyone and although your suggestions are welcome, the final word will be the homilist's.

General Intercessions

Discuss them in class or in your catechetical sessions and include the children's petitions as much as possible. Use the suggested format and catechize the children about what should be prayed and why. These are *general* intercessions. Any particular petitions can be prayed in the classroom or at other prayer services.

Presentation and Preparation of the Gifts

This part of the liturgy has in the past been referred to as the "offertory." However, that title is not correct. For thirty years (ever since Vatican II), the proper title has been "the presentation and preparation of the gifts," or for the sake of liturgical simplicity, the "gifts procession."

What are these gifts? They are bread and wine *only* (and at times gifts for the poor—money, food, clothing). This is not, and never has been, the time to bring up "symbolic" gifts, that is, gifts that are not really gifts at all because they are taken back when Mass is over.

Symbolic representations of what you want to emphasize might be more suitable as part of the introductory rites.

Here is what the *General Instruction of the Roman Missal* has to say: "At the beginning of the liturgy of the eucharist the gifts, which will become Christ's body and blood, are brought to the altar... This is also the time to receive money or other gifts for the church or the poor brought by the faithful or collected at the Mass. These are to be put in a suitable place but not on the altar" (49).

So you see that the gifts we bring up are the gifts that will be transformed.

You may also consider a few accompanying elements, such as dressing the altar as part of the gifts procession. Dressing the altar serves as a delineation between the general intercessions and the gifts procession.

If the altar is being dressed, the children carrying the altar cloth and the corporal (or even flowers—just be sure that they are not placed on the altar) follow directly behind the cross and the candles. The children bringing up the gifts follow a distance behind them and wait at the foot of the altar while the altar is being dressed.

Preface and Eucharistic Prayer

You should be singing all of the acclamations that are included in the eucharistic prayer. You will most often be using the eucharistic prayers for children. Now, will you choose the prayer or will the presider choose it? Be sure this is all taken care of on your planning sheet. Will the presider call "the class in charge" around the altar for the eucharistic prayer? If so, rehearse the children well and have them approach the altar with reverence.

Once they have made a semicircle around the altar (so they don't obstruct the assembly's view of the altar), the children should fold their hands and keep their attention on what the presider is doing.

The Great Amen

The Great Amen is the final element of the eucharistic prayer, but at times we see it falling over into the communion rite. Many times the Great Amen is sung as people are standing up and holding hands and moving their bodies across the church in preparation for the Our Father. The Great Amen is an affirmation of what has just been said, not a preparation for the Our Father. One action should be completed before another is begun.

The Lord's Prayer

In praying the Our Father, you may have the children do what is customary—hold hands, use the Orans position, or just keep their hands folded. There is no mandated way to pray the Our Father—other than standing up. Just make sure that everyone is doing the same thing.

Sign of Peace

Help to make the sign of peace mean something by asking the children to concentrate on the people directly on either side of them. Go over this in the classroom or in your catechetical sessions. You can create an exercise in which the children make a heartfelt wish for peace in everyone's life.

Post-communion

After communion, for this liturgy, you might want to include a prayer or a song—but not at the expense of silence. You have given the children reason to expect silence after communion. Now that they know what to do with silence, keep it always in the forefront. Now and then you might want to include something else, if the liturgy calls for it.

What is your recessional song? Try not to let this moment slip away by including a song that the children aren't familiar with. Engage their attention until the very end by choosing a song they know and love. The song will resound throughout the church as the children sing with energy and enthusiasm.

One caution from the *Directory for Masses with Children*: "Some rites should never be adapted for children lest the difference between Masses with children and Masses with adults become too pronounced. These are the acclamations and the responses to the priest's greeting, the Lord's prayer, and the Trinitarian formulary at the end of the blessing with which the priest concludes the Mass" (39).

A Quick Guide to Planning Sheet 2

- Choose the readings.

- Choose the music.

- Choose the readers.

- Choose the gifts procession people.

- Choose the altar servers and the acolytes.

- Fill out the liturgy planning sheet. Give a copy to the presider.

- Speak with the presider and ask for his ideas.

- Discuss and write the general intercessions with the children.

- Rehearse. Rehearse readings, responses, acclamations, songs.

- Rehearse gathering around the altar and the sign of peace. Rehearse going up to communion. Rehearse silence.

Being comfortable with the ritual and knowing what comes next actually frees the mind to experience all that can be experienced in liturgy. Take the time in your sessions to explain the liturgical prayers, their ancient (or not-so-ancient roots) and how it is true that "from age to age you gather a people to yourself." If you do not have all of this information, ask someone who does to speak to the children.

Feel free to make notes on the back of the planning sheet if you are including other elements and rituals. Using the back of the sheet is better than writing on another sheet, which is bound to go astray. It is a good idea when you are running off your planning sheet to run it on colored paper. That way it can be picked out of the stack of papers that it's bound to end up in.

Part III

Fully Initiated

Now is the time that you feel confident in what you are doing. Now is the time that you know the options, adaptations, additions, and subtractions that can be a part of the liturgy. Now is the time to be very careful.

Just because you know what can be done and how to do it and where it should be done, should you do it? Sometimes the tendency is to add all the whistles and bells and incense that are allowed. But is bigger really better? Or do you suppose that less is more? That is up to you to decide.

Now that your liturgical sense is well developed, consider a few more thought-provoking topics.

Who Should Proclaim Scripture During Liturgy with Children?

This is what the *Directory for Masses with Children* has to say: "For this reason as many children as possible should have special parts in the celebration: for example … proclaiming the readings …" (22). In addition, "When the text of the readings lends itself to this, it may be helpful to have the children read it with parts distributed among them, as is provided for the reading of the Lord's passion during Holy Week" (47).

Recently, however, there has been some doubt as to whether children in kindergarten, first, and second grades should proclaim Scripture. The argument is that the required level of understanding is not there. Others counter that there is always some level of understanding and that understanding continues to develop throughout our lives.

What should probably be foremost in our minds is that the children should not be showcased. They should be chosen because they possess certain gifts that will lead to proper proclamation. They should be taught to pray Scripture. The level of understanding must begin somewhere.

If you feel that liturgy would best be served by not having the young "class in charge" proclaim the word, you might want to consider a teacher, a sibling, or an older member of the "brother-sister" class as a Scripture reader. That is something for you to pray and discern.

We're Surrounded by Environment

When you plan your liturgical environment, there are two questions you must ask yourself: (1) Does the environment serve the paschal mystery? and (2) Is the church decorated like a classroom? The answers, of course, should be yes and no, respectively.

The life, death, and resurrection of Jesus Christ should be foremost in your mind when you are planning the liturgical environment. You will have a focus for your liturgy, which could be a saint's day, a celebration of the sacraments, Religious Education Day, or Catholic Schools Week. Be mindful of what you do with these.

You should pay special attention to where you're going to place the visuals. For instance, a beautiful altar should not be covered up with butcher paper and drawings. If you would like visuals in which everyone has participated, think of placing them somewhere in the worship space—on an easel, on a pillar, at the bottom of the altar steps, anywhere that would not hide the noble simplicity of the furnishings.

After the liturgy, take some of the visual elements you used and put them somewhere on the school grounds, the hall, the school building, or in a classroom. Your particular liturgy celebrating Religious Education Day or Catholic Schools Week, for example, does not apply to the other liturgies being celebrated that day or that week. Post your banners elsewhere.

Visuals that are used in the children's liturgy should be intrinsic to the liturgy itself. "The liturgy of the Mass contains many visual elements and these should be given great prominence with children. This is especially true of the particular visual elements in the course of the liturgical year, for example, the veneration of the cross, the Easter candle, the lights on the feast of the Presentation of the Lord, and the variety of colors and liturgical appointments. It is appropriate to introduce other elements that will permit children to perceive visually the wonderful works of God in creation and redemption and thus support their prayer. For the same reason, the use of art work prepared by the children themselves may be useful, for example, as illustrations of a homily, as visual expressions of the intentions of the general intercessions, or as inspirations to reflection" (*Directory for Masses with Children* 35, 36).

One of the ways to connect liturgy and life is to relate what has happened in the church to what is happening in the lives of the children. What is appropriate in the classroom or catechetical session is not always appropriate in the church, but the two are related and both can be celebrated. Use your good sense of what belongs where; you have it and will continue to develop it.

Of Music, Servers, and Communion Ministers

Your musical sense should be fairly well honed by now insofar as choosing music for children's liturgies is concerned. You know what music they know and you know what music they like. There should be a repertoire of appropriate songs, including service music. If your music minister selects the songs, become familiar with them yourself. The acclamations, of course, are always sung, and songs are added to the known list periodically. It is important that the children know the songs well and are enthusiastic about them because that adds greatly to the liturgy. The songs found in your music issue should be given first consideration, since they are the songs that the children will sing on Sunday, along with the rest of the assembly.

Acolytes and altar servers can be trained to model liturgical responses If their remarks to you include the fact that no one in the assembly is responding, remind them that people need to see the servers respond, so they know to respond as well. Teach the servers to sing and respond appropriately during the liturgy.

Who has been serving as communion ministers? Are they teachers in the school or catechists in the religious education program? You might think of expanding this ministry to include parents or other interested people. You might even consider including some former students. There might be people whose children have graduated from the school or religious education program and who would like to keep in touch by participating in this manner. There are many parish people who would be honored to be included as participants in a children's liturgy. Give them that opportunity. If you are shorthanded, ask the communion ministers on the parish list.

Sometimes just looking around at who attends a regular children's liturgy will give you a clue about who would like to participate. One of your children's liturgies could include the blessing of these ministers.

You can address every aspect of the liturgy if you take things one step at a time. Do not expect everything to be perfect (according to your way of looking at it) when you are first starting out. It is as perfect as it needs to be at that particular time. The elements mentioned in this chapter are refinements that you can address when you are comfortable with everything else.

This final part assumes that you are planning a wonderful liturgical celebration for, perhaps, the school's one hundredth anniversary, with all of the children and many parishioners in attendance. Follow the liturgy planning sheet and see what develops.

Some Suggestions and Advice

- Discuss environment with those who are planning the celebration with you. Develop ideas.

- Choose readings and music. For a celebration such as this, you would probably have a committee. In that case, although the readings would be in your area of expertise, the music minister should speak with the committee regarding the songs that are chosen.

- Choose ministers (readers, gifts procession people, altar servers, communion ministers).

- Fill out the liturgy planning sheet and give it to the presider. Perhaps the presider would like to meet with the entire committee and help to plan and develop the celebration.

Gathering Song and Procession

When choosing an appropriate piece of music, consider the rhythm. Can people move to it? Would people in the procession move in time with the music? Who will you include in the procession? Think carefully on who should be included and if you would like them to move in time with the music. It doesn't have to be a "liturgical dance" as we know it; instead, you could use gestures or movements that can be done by "regular" people.

Consider a Sprinkling Rite

This would be a good time to dip a large-size branch (juniper is good) into the water and make it even a little more than a sprinkle.

Gloria

Since you are planning for a special celebration, you might sing the Gloria. "The Gloria is sung or said on Sundays outside Advent and Lent, on solemnities and feasts, and in special, more solemn celebrations" (*General Instruction of the Roman Missal* 31).

Readings

You have chosen the readings. Now, how would you like to approach them? We have seen before that they can be proclaimed in dialogue form, as in the Lord's passion. Do the dialogue if it seems appropriate. Never include something just to be different—and you must be honest with yourself.

There are several ways in which the psalm can be approached. Certainly, the psalm should be sung. It could be sung antiphonally or in the more usual responsorial form.

According to the *Directory for Masses with Children*, "Verses of psalms, carefully selected in accord with the understanding of children, or singing in the form of psalmody or the Alleluia with a simple verse should be sung between the readings. The children should always have a part in this singing, but sometimes reflective silence may be substituted for the singing" (46).

There may be a second reading, but think that option over carefully—especially if you have used dialogue options for the first reading. Do not stuff the liturgy just because you can.

Sing all of the acclamations; the Gospel acclamation is the first.

The presider or deacon will proclaim the Gospel, but will he preach the homily? "With the consent of the pastor or rector of the church, one of the adults may speak to the children after the gospel, especially if the priest finds it difficult to adapt himself to the mentality of children..." (*Directory for Masses with Children* 24).

Creed

Will you pray the Creed? It can be either recited or sung. Be careful not to act it out or perform it in a way that overshadows what came before and what will come after.

General Intercessions

General intercessions can be accompanied by a sung response, or they can be sung entirely. They also can be accompanied by visual elements.

Gifts Procession

Dressing the altar is something you might want to consider in this celebration.

Let everyone who has a part in this procession wait until all rituals are accomplished. They would then return to their seats at the same time.

Eucharistic Prayer

Plan to sing all the acclamations in the eucharistic prayer. Remember to finish singing the Great Amen before getting ready for the Our Father. Complete one action before another is begun.

Lord's Prayer

How is the Our Father prayed? Is it sung, chanted, or recited? There are reasons for each, but you must choose the one that works best with that particular liturgy.

Communion Procession

Think of the time of going to share communion as a procession. Sometimes just the approach to something makes us look at it in a different way. If this part of the Mass is thought of as "going to communion," that is fine. But if it is thought of as the Body of Christ in procession, joining together to celebrate the mystery of the Eucharist, that is even better.

Post-communion

Once again, is silence your plan for the prayer after communion? Or would this be the time you would like to insert a special song to commemorate this celebration. Be sure it is a song of praise that everyone can join in singing.

Once you have given a copy of the planning sheet to the presider, schedule some time to speak with him about the liturgy. This liturgy requires the input of everyone who has a role in bringing the celebration to the assembly.

Help and More Help

There is help out there, you have only to take advantage of it. The following books are ones that you must have close at hand.

The Lectionary for Masses with Children

You have been using this all along. If you have been borrowing one and need to purchase one of your own (for the school or program) or if you are just starting out and you are a first-time user, here are a few points to consider. There are several different "editions" of the *Lectionary for Masses with Children*. The texts in the books are the same, but their setup varies from publisher to publisher. You can purchase a book with all the Sunday and all the weekday readings. Or you can purchase one with Sundays only and weekdays only. Or you can purchase one set up in the different cycles. Look them all over and select the book that best suits your needs.

Directory for Masses with Children

The *Directory for Masses with Children* is included in Appendix C. You can also buy it as part of a collection titled *The Liturgy Documents: A Parish Resource* (Liturgy Training Publications). It is probably best to buy the entire *Liturgy Documents* collection, because you will be referring to them for such elements as music, environment, and everything you need to know about liturgy. They will be there if you need them; once you become comfortable with the *Directory for Masses with Children*, you will be eager to learn more.

Ordo

The *Order of Prayer in the Liturgy of the Hours and Celebration of the Eucharist* (Paulist Press) has not been mentioned because most likely you would not have needed it before now. The *Ordo* gives you the readings of the day, the liturgical color to be worn, and all the information contained in its title. The *Ordo* is a small book, usually kept in the sacristy for quick reference, but you should have one of your own. The price is nominal. Remember that the *Ordo* contains more weekday readings than the *Lectionary for Masses with Children*, so do not try to match them up day by day.

Sharing the Light of Faith and The Mystery of Faith

Sharing the Light of Faith (United States Catholic Conference) and *The Mystery of Faith* (Federation of Diocesan Liturgical Commissions) are foundational books that you should become well acquainted with.

Book of Blessings

The *Book of Blessings* (Catholic Book Publishing Company) should also be numbered among the books in your liturgical library. This book contains blessings for every occasion. It is nice to include a blessing at times during the liturgy: for instance, a blessing of rosaries on an appropriate day, a blessing of new sacred vessels, or a blessing of someone who is leaving the school.

These basic books should be on the shelf of any school or religious education program. Include them in your budget.

They are your liturgical textbooks from which the spiritual experience will flow.

Summary

It is now time to take what you have experienced in the liturgy and put it into action. What did you bring to the liturgy and what are you taking away? Will you act on what you have experienced? Will you bring that and more to the next liturgy?

You now know the basics of planning and developing Masses with children. That is what this book hoped to accomplish. It is a practical handbook that will soon become second nature to you and will allow for spiritual development and a real sense of the sacred to all in the assembly.

Now go back to Part I.

Appendix A

Liturgy Planning Sheets

When you know absolutely nothing about planning a children's liturgy, trust this ...

LITURGY PLANNING SHEET 1

Date _____ Time _____ Group _____

Presider _____ Occasion _____

(These are the only elements you have to concern yourself with.)

I. INTRODUCTORY RITES

Gathering song _____

II. LITURGY OF THE WORD

Choose from seasonal readings in the children's lectionary.

First reading   Read by: _____

Response   Read/sung by: _____

Gospel

Intercessions   Read by: _____
1. For needs of the church
2. For public authorities and the salvation of the world
3. For those oppressed by any need
4. For the local community
5. For specifics in your celebration

III. LITURGY OF THE EUCHARIST

Gifts procession
(2 persons carrying
bread and wine) _____ _____

Gifts song _____

(*Two options follow:* It is good to have sung acclamations. Your music teacher can choose. You may want to have Father gather the children around the altar for the eucharistic prayer.)

IV. COMMUNION RITE

Communion song _____
Song after communion _____

V. CONCLUDING RITE

Recessional song _____

Other personnel: Cross and candle bearers, altar servers, communion ministers.

LITURGY PLANNING SHEET 2

Date _____ Time _____ Group _____

Presider _____ Occasion _____

I. INTRODUCTORY RITE

Gathering song

Penitential rite

Opening prayer

II. LITURGY OF THE WORD

First reading   Read by: _____

Response   Read/sung by: _____

Gospel acclamation (sung)
Gospel and homily

General intercessions   Read by: _____

III. LITURGY OF THE EUCHARIST

Presentation and preparation
 of the gifts (2 persons)   _____   _____

Song   _____

Preface and eucharistic prayer
Holy, Holy (sung acclamations)
Memorial acclamation
Amen

IV. COMMUNION RITE

Our Father
Doxology
Sign of Peace
Breaking of the bread
Communion song   _____

Prayer/song after communion

V. CONCLUDING RITE

Blessing and dismissal
Recessional song   _____

GENERAL INSTRUCTIONS

Acolytes

Altar servers

Music

LITURGY PLANNING SHEET 3
for Eucharistic Liturgy (Mass)

Date _____ Time _____ Group _____

Presider _____ Occasion _____

(Optional elements are in parentheses. Choose/select as appropriate.)

I. INTRODUCTORY RITE

Gathering song _____

Penitential rite
or sprinkling rite _____

(Gloria) _____

Opening prayer _____

II. LITURGY OF THE WORD

Reading one _____

Response _____

(Reading two) _____

Gospel acclamation
Gospel _____

Homily _____

(Creed) _____

General intercessions _____

III. LITURGY OF THE EUCHARIST

Presentation and
preparation of gifts _____

Song _____

Preface and
eucharistic prayer _____

Holy, Holy, Holy _____

Memorial acclamation _____

Great Amen _____

(over)

IV. COMMUNION RITE

Our Father _____

Doxology _____

Sign of peace _____

Breaking of
  bread/Lamb of God _____

Communion _____

Communion song _____

Song after communion _____

Prayer after communion _____

V. CONCLUDING RITE

Blessing and dismissal _____

Recessional song _____

PERSONNEL

Planning leader: _____

Presider: _____

Altar servers: _____

Music coordinator/leader: _____

Environment
  coordinator/sacristan: _____

Ministers of hospitality: _____

Communion ministers: _____

Lectors: _____

Notes for Liturgical Environment

Notes for Liturgy of the Word/Readings

Notes for Presider or Homilist

Appendix B

Celebrations Throughout the Year

Does your school or religious education program celebrate a liturgy on a certain day of the week? every week? every month? Why? If that last question brings you up short, it was meant to. Is there some tradition in your school that calls for a liturgy at a certain time of a certain day? Have you examined the reason for that lately?

You may be missing some glorious celebrations by limiting yourself to a certain day. The time may not be negotiable due to schedules that must be met or the unavailability of a presider later in the day, but you might want to rethink the day.

Take a look at the liturgical calendar (the one from your parish that you always have handy) and run through the saint's days, designated days on the secular calendar, days that the pope or bishops have named as special days. Think of what can be done with them, how to celebrate them liturgically. Let us start at the beginning of the school year (because that is the sequence in which the liturgies are planned) and see what unfolds.

Choose a focus for your year. Consider celebrating seasons, both earth seasons and liturgical seasons. See how they fit with one other. Consider celebrating saint's days or major secular days to show that liturgy and life are one. Consider recognizing and celebrating ministries and organizations within your parish. Connect saints and ministries. Bless those in ministry during the liturgy (see *Book of Blessings*). Make certain that there is continuity. Do not try to stuff everything into one year; pull back and construct the year. Look through the *Lectionary for Masses with Children* and choose the emphasis for the entire school year.

September

School opens and everyone is full of enthusiasm. A Mass of the Holy Spirit would be appropriate or one for the opening of the school year (see *Lectionary for Masses with Children*.) Be careful at the gifts procession. This is one of the times when a "many-items" procession used to take place. Remember, only bread and wine are to be taken up. Gifts for the poor probably would not be a consideration at this time because there has not been time to collect food or other items.

The birth of Mary is celebrated on September 8, which may be an appropriate way to begin the school year. "Beginnings" would be a good focus. Use the readings of the day and choose music that would emphasize acceptance of God's will and music praising God. Limit yourself to one or two Marian hymns.

October

October offers many choices. Decide which day most emphasizes the theme of your year.

Here are two choices in as many days: October 1, the Memorial of St. Thérèse of Lisieux and October 2, the Memorial of the Guardian Angels. Select songs that bring out the character of the day. What is it that defines St. Thérèse most? What do we want to say about God and angels?

The next week presents us with the Memorial of Our Lady of the Rosary on October 7. This is the time to bless rosaries and perhaps to honor the people in the parish's rosary society (or whatever the name of the group may be). Look to the *Book of Blessings* for a rosary blessing and a blessing for the people who promote the praying of the rosary.

October 15 brings the day honoring St. Teresa of Avila, who is a doctor of the church. What is a doctor of the church? Why was St. Teresa named one? Take the opportunity to learn the answer to these questions in the days *before* the liturgy. That way, during the liturgy, you can experience what happens because of the facts you've already learned.

Have you yet encountered your parish name day? It could be American Martyrs on October 19. Even if it is not, you might like to recognize and honor some of the people who began the church in America.

November

November 1 is the Solemnity of All Saints; November 2 is All Souls Day. For the eucharistic celebration on the holy day (All Saints), list the "saint" of each child and chant those names during the entrance procession. The homily, as permitted in the documents, could be given by a lay person. This would be an opportunity for a few people to tell the story of how having their particular saint's name has affected their lives. This could tie in nicely with the Gospel of the day, the Beatitudes.

November 2 could be marked with a prayer service where children call out the names of people they know who have died during the past year. You could begin the ceremony by lighting candles and use the readings of the day. The names of anyone else who has died—such as grandparents, aunts, uncles, those who have died more than a year ago—could be written down and put in a container beside a candle that is kept lighted during the day. (*Note on candles:* Although long tapers are beautiful, it is better to use small votives or a votive in a bowl-shaped container in a liturgy with children. It is safer if the flame is recessed.)

What could you do with your Thanksgiving service that would lead to your parish's Thanksgiving liturgy? The celebration could begin the day before Thanksgiving for the sake of convenience. Perhaps a food collection from the children could be brought to the parish liturgy. This food could be held and distributed to the poor between Thanksgiving and Christmas, which is only a few weeks. Or the children could bring from home a representation of their Thanksgiving dinner—a basket with bread or ears of corn and fruit. They could fix this basket and decorate it and bring it to Mass the next day to be blessed. The baskets could be carried up in the entrance procession and placed in the sanctuary area to be blessed after the homily.

December

In December, the Advent liturgy is a joyful anticipation of Christ's coming. It is linked to the joyful anticipation of giving gifts to people and anticipating the happiness those gifts will bring. The "secular" hustle and bustle before Christmas is not all bad, especially when it is related to giving, not receiving. What we learn in the readings is part of our lives. What did John the Baptist do? He announced the coming of Jesus. We can do the same. Jesus gives himself to us; we give ourselves to others. The mind-set makes all the difference in the world.

One of the early December feasts is St. Nicholas Day, December 6. Do you dare emphasize St. Nicholas over Santa Claus? How many seasonal drawings of St. Nicholas do you have hung in the children's spaces? Perhaps you could tell the story of St. Nicholas and ask the children from other countries, or children who have parents from other countries, if they had ever heard of Santa Claus before they came here. What is their equivalent of Santa Claus and when do they celebrate gift-giving?

December 8 is the Solemnity of the Immaculate Conception of the Virgin Mary. Seeing Our Lady as patroness of the entire United States, you can pray for our government, for good moral leaders, for the students who will be growing up to lead the world. All this can be prayed in the general intercessions.

December 12 is the Feast of Our Lady of Guadalupe, the patroness of the Americas. All of the Americas join together to honor Our Lady of Guadalupe. Use the high-tech knowledge that is available and look for Our Lady of Guadalupe on the Internet. Use what you learn to create a collage of words describing what happened to Juan Diego as the courier of news of Our Lady of Guadalupe.

January

Depending upon when sessions start up again after Christmas vacation, there are three or four saints (and one "blessed") that you can celebrate. On these occasions you could sing Christmas songs because until the Baptism of Our Lord, it is still the Christmas season.

The second week in January is Vocation Awareness Week. Would you like to celebrate it with a eucharistic liturgy? There are special readings and prayers in the lectionary and sacramentary for vocations. In addition to the priest telling his story during the homily, a religious sister and brother can tell theirs. In addition, married people can be included; reach out to other vocations as well.

Everyone celebrates Martin Luther King Jr. Day, either on the actual day of his birth or some time on the three-day weekend. In remembrance of a man who acted on behalf of peace and justice, we can commemorate the ideals for which he worked. A liturgy for peace and justice (in the lectionary and the sacramentary) would be appropriate. To add action to those prayers would show that you really mean what you pray. How can you show your support for those who are working to bring about justice in our time?

February

February offers many wonderful days to celebrate. The Feast of the Presentation of Our Lord (Candlemas Day) is one of the first days—February 2. This is the day that candles to be used during the entire year are blessed. A number of ceremonies can be developed in which this is done. If your blessing takes place during Mass, bring the candles up in the entrance procession, place them to the side of the altar on a previously prepared table. They can be blessed after the homily, using the rite from the *Book of Blessings*.

The next day, February 3, is the feast of St. Blase. Use the rite in the *Book of Blessings* for the blessing of throats and tell one of the legends of St. Blase. Make this legend-telling part of the prayer service before throats are blessed.

President's Day, a civic holiday to be sure, but one that should be celebrated in a day of prayer, can be celebrated on many days surrounding the birthday of Abraham Lincoln or George Washington. The actually designated President's Day is usually a school holiday, but the catalyst for this day came from these two presidents' birthdays. Let your imagination run wild as you celebrate this day all over the school. Include a eucharistic liturgy and pray for all who have been presidents of the United States, as well as for the United States itself and its present administration.

Ash Wednesday will occur sometime in February and Lent will begin. Celebrate a liturgy on Ash Wednesday. Do not just "give out" ashes as if some type of magical symbolism were attached to them. Put the ritual in its proper context, and emphasize the words that are part of it. Liturgy is always the first consideration. Accentuate fasting (in all ways), praying, and almsgiving and how these are to be carried out during the season.

March

During Lent, two days that are faithfully observed in many parishes are St. Patrick's Day on March 17 and St. Joseph's Day on March 19. It is a challenge to give both of these saints their due, since they fall within two days of each other. Choose one of the days to celebrate a Mass and choose the other day to have a prayer service. You could alternate the services in succeeding years.

April

Easter vacation probably will fall during the first part of April. When everyone returns, it will be time to plan for Earth Day on April 25. Use the readings "For Productive Land and After the Harvest" and put into action a plan that will renew the earth all year long.

May

Do you usually plan a May crowning of Mary? This would be a good time for a glorious procession, wherever one can be accommodated, around and into the church. Schedule it for a day in May when there are no feasts or memorials. There are many days in the first part of May when a crowning could be put on your calendar.

On Memorial Day we honor all those women and men who have died in the service of our country—in wars, conflicts, police actions—whatever name one gives to armed tragedies. List those you know who have died under these circumstances. Pray, too, that there will be no more wars and fighting. Discuss with the children what we can do now to begin to make certain that the future leaders will be the ones to bring about peace.

June

It is June already. Hold a Mass of farewell, hoping that all will fare well during the summer days. There is a Mass for the end of the school year in the lectionary. The Feast of St. Anthony of Padua is on June 13 and the Feast of the Sacred Heart of Jesus is on June 19. Perhaps your final liturgy will be held on one of those days.

July, August

Include in your end-of-summer letter a Fourth of July prayer and a reminder of the Feast of the Assumption on August 15. Encourage families to consider these two school-free months as an extension of the prayer life begun in the previous school year and as a time of preparation for all that is to come.

Appendix C

Directory for Masses With Children

INTRODUCTION

1.   The Church must show special concern for baptized children who have yet to be fully initiated through the sacraments of confirmation and eucharist as well as for children who have only recently been admitted to holy communion. Today the circumstances in which children grow up are not favorable to their spiritual progress.[1] In addition parents sometimes scarcely fulfill the obligations they accepted at the baptism of their children to bring them up as Christians.

2.   In the upbringing of children in the Church a special difficulty arises from the fact that liturgical celebrations, especially the eucharist, cannot fully exercise their inherent pedagogical force upon children.[2] Although the vernacular may now be used at Mass, still the words and signs have not been sufficiently adapted to the capacity of children.

In fact, even in daily life children do not always understand all their experiences with adults but rather may find them boring. It cannot therefore be expected of the liturgy that everything must always be intelligible to them. Nonetheless, we may fear spiritual harm if over the years children repeatedly experience in the Church things that are barely comprehensible: recent psychological study has established how profoundly children are formed by the religious experience of infancy and early childhood, because of the special religious receptivity proper to those years.[3]

3.   The Church follows its Master, who "put his arms around the children ... and blessed them" (Mk 10:16). It cannot leave children in the condition described. Vatican Council II had spoken in the Constitution on the Liturgy about the need of liturgical adaptation for various groups.[4] Soon afterwards, especially in the first Synod of

Bishops held in Rome in 1967, the Church began to consider how participation by children could be easier. On the occasion of the Synod, the President of the Consilium for the Implementation of the Constitution on the Liturgy said explicitly that it could not be a matter of "creating some entirely special rite but rather of retaining, shortening, or omitting some elements or of making a better selection of texts."[5]

4.   All the details of eucharistic celebration with a congregation were determined in the General Instruction of the revised Roman Missal published in 1969. Then this Congregation began to prepare a special Directory for Masses with Children, as a supplement to the General Instruction. This was done in response to repeated petitions from the entire Catholic world and with the cooperation of men and women specialists from almost every nation.

5.   Like the *General Instruction of the Roman Missal*, this Directory reserves some adaptations to the conference of bishops or to individual bishops.[6]

Some adaptations of the Mass may be necessary for children in a given country but cannot be included in a general directory. In accord with the *Constitution on the Liturgy* art. 40, the conferences of bishops are to propose such adaptations to the Apostolic See for introduction into the liturgy with its consent.

6.   The Directory is concerned with children who have not yet entered the period of preadolescence. It does not speak directly of children who are physically or mentally handicapped, because a broader adaptation is sometimes necessary for them.[7] Nevertheless, the following norms may also be applied to the handicapped, with the necessary changes.

7.   The first chapter of the Directory (nos. 8–15) gives a kind of foundation by considering the different ways in which children are introduced to the eucharistic liturgy. The second chapter briefly treats Masses with adults in which children also take part (nos. 16–19). Finally, the third chapter (nos. 20–54) treats at greater length Masses with children in which only some adults take part.

CHAPTER I
THE INTRODUCTION OF CHILDREN TO THE EUCHARISTIC CELEBRATION

8.   A fully Christian life is inconceivable without participation in the liturgical services in which the faithful, gathered into a single assembly, celebrate the paschal mystery. Therefore, the religious initiation of children must be in harmony with this purpose.[8] The Church baptizes children and therefore, relying on the gifts conferred by this sacrament, it must be concerned that once baptized they grow in communion with Christ and each other. The sign and pledge of that communion is participation in the eucharistic table, for which children are being prepared or led to a deeper realization of its meaning. This liturgical and eucharistic formation may not be separated from their general education, both human and Christian; indeed it would be harmful if their liturgical formation lacked such a basis.

9.   For this reason all who have a part in the formation of children should consult and work together toward one objective: that even if children already have some feeling for God and the things of God, they may also experience in proportion to their age and personal development the human values that are present in the eucharistic celebration. These values include the community activity, exchange of greetings, capacity to listen and to seek and grant pardon, expression of gratitude, experience of symbolic actions, a meal of friendship, and festive celebration.[9]

Eucharistic catechesis, dealt with in no. 12, should develop such human values. Then, depending on their age and their psychological and social situation, children will gradually open their minds to the perception of Christian values and the celebration of the mystery of Christ.[10]

10.   The Christian family has the greatest role in instilling these Christian and human values.[11] Thus Christian education, provided by parents and other educators, should be strongly encouraged in relation to the liturgical formation of children as well.

By reason of the duty in conscience freely accepted at the baptism of their children, parents are bound to teach them gradually how to pray. This they do by praying with them each day and by introducing them to prayers said privately.[12] If children, prepared in this way even from their early years, take part in the Mass with their family when they wish, they will easily begin to sing and to pray in the liturgical community and indeed will already have some initial idea of the eucharistic mystery.

If the parents are weak in faith but still wish their children to receive Christian formation, they should be urged at least to communicate to their children the human values mentioned already and, when the occasion arises, to participate in meetings of parents and in noneucharistic celebrations held with children.

11.   The Christian communities to which the individual families belong or in which the children live also have a responsibility toward children baptized in the Church. By giving witness to the Gospel, living communal charity, and actively celebrating the mysteries of Christ, the Christian community is an excellent school of Christian and liturgical formation for the children who live in it.

Within the Christian community, godparents or other persons noted for their dedicated service can, out of apostolic zeal, contribute greatly to the necessary catechesis in the case of families that fail in their obligation toward the children's Christian upbringing.

Preschool programs, Catholic schools, and various kinds of associations for children serve these same ends in a special way.

12.   Even in the case of children, the liturgy itself always exerts its own inherent power to instruct.[13] Yet within religious-education programs in the schools and parishes the necessary importance should be given to catechesis on the Mass.[14] This catechesis should be directed to the child's active, conscious, and authentic participation.[15] "Suited to children's age and capabilities, it should, by means of the main rites and prayers of the Mass, aim at conveying its meaning, including what relates to taking part in the Church's life."[16] This is especially true of the text of the eucharistic prayer and of the acclamations by which the children take part in this prayer.

The catechesis preparing children for first communion calls for special mention. In it they should learn not only the truths of faith regarding the eucharist but also how from first communion on—after being prepared according to their capacity by penance—they can as full members of Christ's Body take part actively with the people of God in the eucharist, sharing in the Lord's table and the community of their brothers and sisters.

13. Various kinds of celebrations may also play a major role in the liturgical formation of children and in their preparation for the Church's liturgical life. By the very fact of such celebrations children easily come to appreciate some liturgical elements, for example, greetings, silence, and common praise (especially when this is sung together). But care must by taken that the instructive element does not become dominant in these celebrations.

14. Depending on the capacity of the children, the word of God should have a greater and greater place in these celebrations. In fact, as the children's spiritual capacity develops, celebrations of the word of God in the strict sense should be held frequently, especially during Advent and Lent.[17] These will help greatly to develop in the children an appreciation of the word of God.

15. While all that has been said remains true, the final purpose of all liturgical and eucharistic formation must be a greater and greater conformity to the Gospel in the daily life of the children.

CHAPTER II
MASSES WITH ADULTS IN WHICH CHILDREN ALSO PARTICIPATE

16. In many places parish Masses are celebrated, especially on Sundays and holy days, at which a good many children take part along with the large number of adults. On such occasions the witness of adult believers can have a great effect upon the children. Adults can in turn benefit spiritually from experiencing the part that the children have within the Christian community. The Christian spirit of the family is greatly fostered when children take part in these Masses together with their parents and other family members.

Infants who as yet are unable or unwilling to take part in the Mass may be brought in at the end of Mass to be blessed together with the rest of the community. This may be done, for example, if parish helpers have been taking care of them in a separate area.

17. Nevertheless, in Masses of this kind it is necessary to take great care that the children present do not feel neglected because of their inability to participate or to understand what happens and what is proclaimed in the celebration. Some account should be taken of their presence: for example, by speaking to them directly in the introductory

comments (as at the beginning and the end of Mass) and at some point in the homily.

Sometimes, moreover, if the place itself and the nature of the community permit, it will be appropriate to celebrate the liturgy of the word, including a homily, with the children in a separate, but not too distant, room. Then, before the eucharistic liturgy begins, the children are led to the place where the adults have meanwhile celebrated their own liturgy of the word.

18. It may also be very helpful to give some tasks to the children. They may, for example, bring forward the gifts or perform one or other of the songs of the Mass.

19. If the number of children is large, it may at times be suitable to plan the Mass so that it corresponds more closely to the needs of the children. In this case the homily should be directed to them but in such a way that adults may also benefit from it. Wherever the bishop permits, in addition to the adaptations already provided in the Order of Mass, one or other of the particular adaptations described later in the Directory may be employed in a Mass celebrated with adults in which children also participate.

CHAPTER III
MASSES WITH CHILDREN IN WHICH ONLY A FEW ADULTS PARTICIPATE

20. In addition to the Masses in which children take part with their parents and other family members (which are not always possible everywhere), Masses with children in which only a few adults take part are recommended, especially during the week. From the beginning of the liturgical reform it has been clear to everyone that some adaptations are necessary in these Masses.[18]

Such adaptations, but only those of a more general kind, will be considered later (nos. 38–54).

21. It is always necessary to keep in mind that these eucharistic celebrations must lead children toward the celebration of Mass with adults, especially the Masses at which the Christian community must come together on Sundays.[19] Thus, apart from adaptations that are necessary because of the children's age, the result should not be entirely

special rites, markedly different from the Order of Mass celebrated with a congregation.[20] The purpose of the various elements should always correspond with what is said in the *General Instruction of the Roman Missal* on individual points, even if at times for pastoral reasons an absolute identity cannot be insisted upon.

OFFICES AND MINISTRIES IN THE CELEBRATION

22.   The principles of active and conscious participation are in a sense even more significant for Masses celebrated with children. Every effort should therefore be made to increase this participation and to make it more intense. For this reason as many children as possible should have special parts in the celebration: for example, preparing the place and the altar (see no. 29), acting as cantor (see no. 24), singing in a choir, playing musical instruments (see no. 32), proclaiming the readings (see nos. 24 and 47), responding during the homily (see no. 48), reciting the intentions of the general intercessions, bringing the gifts to the altar, and performing similar activities in accord with the usage of various peoples (see no. 34).

To encourage participation, it will sometimes be helpful to have several additions, for example, the insertion of motives for giving thanks before the priest begins the dialogue of the preface.

In all this, it should be kept in mind that external activities will be fruitless and even harmful if they do not serve the internal participation of the children. Thus religious silence has its importance even in Masses with children (see no. 37). The children should not be allowed to forget that all the forms of participation reach their high point in eucharistic communion, when the body and blood of Christ are received as spiritual nourishment.[21]

23.   It is the responsibility of the priest who celebrates with children to make the celebration festive, familial, and meditative.[22] Even more than in Masses with adults, the priest is the one to create this kind of attitude, which depends on his personal preparation and his manner of acting and speaking with others.

The priest should be concerned above all about the dignity, clarity, and simplicity of his actions and gestures. In speaking to the children he should express himself so that he will be easily understood, while avoiding any childish style of speech.

The free use of introductory comments[23] will lead children to a genuine liturgical participation, but these should be more than mere explanatory remarks.

It will help him to reach the hearts of the children if the priest sometimes expresses the invitations in his own words, for example, at the penitential rite, the prayer over the gifts, the Lord's Prayer, the sign of peace, and communion.

24. Since the eucharist is always the action of the entire ecclesial community, the participation of at least some adults is desirable. These should be present not as monitors but as participants, praying with the children and helping them to the extent necessary.

With the consent of the pastor or rector of the church, one of the adults may speak to the children after the gospel, especially if the priest finds it difficult to adapt himself to the mentality of children. In this matter the norms soon to be issued by the Congregation for the Clergy should be observed.

Even in Masses with children attention is to be paid to the diversity of ministries so that the Mass may stand out clearly as the celebration of a community.[24] For example, readers and cantors, whether children or adults, should be employed. In this way a variety of voices will keep the children from becoming bored.

PLACE AND TIME OF CELEBRATION

25. The primary place for the eucharistic celebration for children is the church. Within the church, however, a space should be carefully chosen, if available, that will be suited to the number of participants. It should be a place where the children can act with a feeling of ease according to the requirements of a living liturgy that is suited to their age.

If the church does not satisfy these demands, it will sometimes be suitable to celebrate the eucharist with children outside a place of worship. But in that case the place chosen should be appropriate and worthy of the celebration.[25]

26. The time of day chosen for Masses with children should correspond to the circumstances of their lives so that they may be most open to hearing the word of God and to celebrating the eucharist.

27. Weekday Mass in which children participate can certainly be celebrated with greater effect and less danger of boredom if it does not take place every day (for example, in boarding schools). Moreover, preparation can be more careful if there is a longer interval between diverse celebrations.

Sometimes it will be preferable to have common prayer, to which the children may contribute spontaneously, or else a common meditation, or a celebration of the word of God. These are ways of continuing the eucharistic celebrations already held and of leading to a deeper participation in subsequent celebrations.

28. When the number of children who celebrate the eucharist together is very great, attentive and conscious participation becomes more difficult. Therefore, if possible, several groups should be formed; these should not be set up rigidly according to age but with regard for the children's progress in religious formation and catechetical preparation.

During the week such groups may be invited to the sacrifice of the Mass on different days.

PREPARATION FOR THE CELEBRATION

29. Each eucharistic celebration with children should be carefully prepared beforehand, especially with regard to the prayers, songs, readings, and intentions of the general intercessions. This should be done in discussion with the adults and with the children who will have a special ministry in these Masses. If possible, some of the children should take part in preparing and ornamenting the place of celebration and preparing the chalice with the paten and the cruets. Presupposing the appropriate internal participation, such activity will help to develop the spirit of community celebration.

SINGING AND MUSIC

30. Singing must be given great importance in all celebrations, but it is to be especially encouraged in every way for Masses celebrated with children, in view of their special affinity for music.[26] The culture of various peoples and the capabilities of the children present should be taken into account.

If possible, the acclamations should be sung by the children rather than recited, especially the acclamations that form part of the eucharistic prayer.

31. To facilitate the children's participation in singing the Gloria, Credo, Sanctus, and Agnus Dei, it is permissible to use with the melodies appropriate vernacular texts, accepted by competent authority, even if these do not correspond exactly to the liturgical texts.[27]

32. The use of "musical instruments can add a great deal" in Masses with children, especially if they are played by the children themselves.[28] The playing of instruments will help to sustain the singing or to encourage the reflection of the children; sometimes in their own fashion instruments express festive joy and the praise of God.

Care should always be taken, however, that the musical accompaniment does not overpower the singing or become a distraction rather than a help to the children. Music should correspond to the purpose intended for the different periods at which it is played during the Mass.

With these precautions and with due and special discretion, recorded music may also be used in Masses with children, in accord with norms established by the conferences of bishops.

GESTURES

33. In view of the nature of the liturgy as an activity of the entire person and in view of the psychology of children, participation by means of gestures and posture should be strongly encouraged in Masses with children, with due regard for age and local customs. Much depends not only on the actions of the priest,[29] but also on the manner in which the children conduct themselves as a community.

If, in accord with the norms of the *General Instruction of the Roman Missal,*[30] a conference of bishops adapts the congregation's actions at Mass to the mentality of a people, it should take the special condition of children into account or should decide on adaptations that are for children only.

34. Among the actions that are considered under this heading, processions and other activities that involve physical participation deserve special mention.

The children's entering in procession with the priest can serve to help them to experience a sense of the communion that is thus being created.[31] The participation of at least some children in the procession with the Book of the Gospels makes clear the presence of Christ announcing the word to his people. The procession of children with the chalice and the gifts expresses more clearly the value and meaning of the preparation of the gifts. The communion procession, if properly arranged, helps greatly to develop the children's devotion.

VISUAL ELEMENTS

35. The liturgy of the Mass contains many visual elements and these should be given great prominence with children. This is especially true of the particular visual elements in the course of the liturgical year, for example, the veneration of the cross, the Easter candle, the lights on the feast of the Presentation of the Lord, and the variety of colors and liturgical appointments.

In addition to the visual elements that belong to the celebration and to the place of celebration, it is appropriate to introduce other elements that will permit children to perceive visually the wonderful works of God in creation and redemption and thus support their prayer. The liturgy should never appear as something dry and merely intellectual.

36. For the same reason, the use of art work prepared by the children themselves may be useful, for example, as illustrations of a homily, as visual expressions of the intentions of the general intercessions, or as inspirations to reflection.

SILENCE

37. Even in Masses with children "silence should be observed at the designated times as part of the celebration"[32] lest too great a place be given to external action. In their own way children are genuinely capable of reflection. They need some guidance, however, so that they will learn how, in keeping with the different moments of the Mass (for example, after the homily or after communion[33]), to recollect themselves, meditate briefly, or praise God and pray to him in their hearts.[34]

Besides this, with even greater care than in Masses with adults, the liturgical texts should be proclaimed intelligibly and unhurriedly, with the necessary pauses.

PARTS OF THE MASS

38. The general structure of the Mass, which "is made up as it were of the liturgy of the word and the liturgy of the eucharist," should always be maintained, as should certain rites to open and conclude the celebration.[35] Within individual parts of the celebration, the adaptations that follow seem necessary if children are truly to experience, in their own way and according to the psychological patterns of childhood, "the mystery of faith ... by means of rites and prayers."[36]

39. Some rites and texts should never be adapted for children lest the difference between Masses with children and the Masses with adults become too pronounced.[37] These are "the acclamations and the responses to the priest's greeting,"[38] the Lord's Prayer, and the Trinitarian formulary at the end of the blessing with which the priest concludes the Mass. It is urged, moreover, that children should become accustomed to the Nicene Creed little by little, the right to use the Apostles' Creed indicated in no. 49 remaining intact.

A. Introductory Rite

40. The introductory rite of Mass has as its purpose "that the faithful coming together take on the form of a community and prepare themselves to listen to God's word and celebrate the eucharist properly."[39] Therefore every effort should be made to create this disposition in the children and not to jeopardize it by any excess of rites in this part of Mass.

It is sometimes proper to omit one or other element of the introductory rite or perhaps to expand one of the elements. There should always be at least some introductory element, which is completed by the opening prayer. In choosing individual elements, care should be taken that each one be used from time to time and that none be entirely neglected.

B. Reading and Explanation of the Word of God

41. Since readings taken from holy Scripture "form the main part of the liturgy of the word,"[40] even in Masses celebrated with children biblical reading should never be omitted.

42. With regard to the number of readings on Sundays and holy days, the decrees of the conferences of bishops are to be observed. If three or even two readings appointed on Sundays or weekdays can be understood by children only with difficulty, it is permissible to read two or only one of them, but the reading of the gospel should never be omitted.

43. If all the readings assigned to the day seem to be unsuited to the capacity of the children, it is permissible to choose readings or a reading either from the *Lectionary of the Roman Missal* or directly from the Bible, but taking into account the liturgical seasons. It is recommended, moreover, that the individual conferences of bishops see to the composition of lectionaries for Masses with children.

If, because of the limited capabilities of the children, it seems necessary to omit one or other verse of a biblical reading, this should be done cautiously and in such a way "that the meaning of the text or the intent and, as it were, style of the Scriptures are not distorted."[41]

44. In the choice of readings the criterion to be followed is the quality rather than the quantity of the texts from the Scriptures. A shorter reading is not as such always more suited to children than a lengthy reading. Everything depends on the spiritual advantage that the reading can bring to the children.

45. In the biblical texts "God is speaking to his people ... and Christ is present to the faithful through his own word."[42] Paraphrases of Scripture should therefore be avoided. On the other hand, the use of translations that may already exist for the catechesis of children and that are accepted by the competent authority is recommended.

46. Verses of psalms, carefully selected in accord with the understanding of children, or singing in the form of psalmody or the *Alleluia* with a simple verse should be sung between the readings. The children should always have a part in this singing, but sometimes a reflective silence may be substituted for the singing.

If only a single reading is chosen, the singing may follow the homily.

47. All the elements that will help explain the readings should be given great consideration so that the children may make the biblical readings their own and may come more and more to appreciate the value of God's word.

Among such elements are the introductory comments that may precede the readings[43] and that by explaining the context or by introducing the text itself help the children to listen better and more fruitfully. The interpretation and explanation of the readings from the Scriptures in the Mass on a saint's day may include an account of the saint's life, not only in the homily but even before the readings in the form of an introduction.

When the text of the readings lends itself to this, it may be helpful to have the children read it with parts distributed among them, as is provided for the reading of the Lord's passion during Holy Week.

48. The homily explaining the word of God should be given great prominence in all Masses with children. Sometimes the homily intended for children should become a dialogue with them, unless it is preferred that they should listen in silence.

49. If the profession of faith occurs at the end of the liturgy of the word, the Apostle's Creed may be used with children, especially because it is part of their catechetical formation.

C. Presidential Prayers

50. The priest is permitted to choose from the Roman Missal texts of presidential prayers more suited to children, so that he may truly associate the children with himself. But he is to take into account the liturgical season.

51. Since these prayers were composed for adult Christians, however, the principle simply of choosing from among them does not serve the purpose of having the children regard the prayers as an expression of their own life and religious experience.[44] If this is the case, the text of prayers of the Roman Missal may be adapted to the needs of children, but this should be done in such a way that, preserving the purpose of the prayer and to some extent its substance as well, the priest avoids anything that is foreign to the literary genre of a presidential prayer, such as moral exhortations or a childish manner of speech.

52. The eucharistic prayer is of the greatest importance in the eucharist celebrated with children because it is the high point of the entire celebration.[45] Much depends on the manner in which the priest proclaims this prayer[46] and on the way the children take part by listening and making their acclamations.

The disposition of mind required for this central part of the celebration and the calm and reverence with which everything is done must make the children as attentive as possible. Their attention should be on the real presence of Christ on the altar under the elements of bread and wine, on his offering, on the thanksgiving through him and with him and in him, and on the Church's offering, which is made during the prayer and by which the faithful offer themselves and their lives with Christ to the eternal Father in the Holy Spirit.

For the present, the four eucharistic prayers approved by the supreme authority for Masses with adults and introduced into liturgical use are to be employed until the Apostolic See makes other provision for Masses with children.

D. Rites before Communion

53. When the eucharistic prayer has ended, the Lord's Prayer, the breaking of bread, and the invitation to communion should always follow,[47] that is, the elements that have the principal significance in the structure of this part of the Mass.

E. Communion and the Following Rites

54. Everything should be done so that the children who are properly disposed and who have already been admitted to the eucharist may go to the holy table calmly and with recollection and thus take part fully in the eucharistic mystery. If possible, there should be singing, suited to the children, during the communion procession.[48]

The comments that precede the final blessing[49] are important in Masses with children. Before they are dismissed they need some repetition and application of what they have heard, but this should be done in a very few words. In particular, this is the appropriate time to express the connection between the liturgy and life.

At least sometimes, depending on the liturgical seasons and different occasions in the children's life, the priest should use more expanded forms of blessing, but at the end should always retain the Trinitarian formulary with the sign of the cross.[50]

* * * * *

55.   The contents of the Directory have as their purpose to help children readily and joyfully to encounter Christ together in the eucharistic celebration and to stand with him in the presence of the Father.[51] If they are formed by conscious and active participation in the eucharistic sacrifice and meal, they should learn day by day, at home and away from home, to proclaim Christ to others among their family and among their peers, by living the "faith, that works through love" (Gal 5:6).

This Directory was prepared by the Congregation for Divine Worship. On 22 October 1973, Pope Paul VI approved and confirmed it and ordered that it be published.

NOTES

1. See GCD 5.

2. See CSL 33.

3. See GCD 78.

4. See CSL 38; also AP.

5. First Synod of Bishops, Liturgy: *Notitiae* 3 (1967) 368.

6. See DMC 19, 32, 33.

7. See Order of Mass with deaf and mute children of German-speaking regions approved, that is, confirmed by CDW, 26 June 1970 (Prot. no. 1546/70).

8. See CSL 14, 19.

9. See GCD 25.

10. See Vatican Council II, Declaration on Christian Education, *Gravissimum educationis*, no. 2.

11. See ibid, 3.

12. See GCD 78.

13. See CSL 33.

14. See EM 14.

15. See GCD 25.

16. See EM 14; GCD 57.

17. See CSL 35, 4.

18. See DMC 3.

19. See CSL 42, 106.

20. See First Synod of Bishops, Liturgy: *Notitiae* (1967) 368.

21. See GI 56.

22. See DMC 37.

23. See GI 11.

24. See CSL 28.

25. See GI 253.

26. See GI 19.

27. See MS 55.

28. MS 62.

29. See DMC 23.

30. See GI 21.

31. See GI 24.

32. GI 23.

33. See EM 38.

34. See GI 23.

35. GI 8.

36. CSL 48.

37. See DMC 21.

38. GI 15.

39. GI 24.

40. GI 33.

41. Lectionary for Mass: Introduction, 1969 edition, no. 7d.

42. GI 33.

43. See GI 11.

44. See Consilium for the Implementation of the Constitution on the Sacred Liturgy, instruction on translations of liturgical texts for celebrations with a congregation, 25 Jan 1969, no. 20: *Notitiae* 5 (1969) 7.

45. GI 54.

46. See DMC 23, 37.

47. See DMC 23.

48. See MS 32.

49. See GI 11.

50. See DMC 39.

51. See RM, Eucharistic Prayer II.

ABBREVIATIONS

Many texts listed here appear in *Documents on the Liturgy, 1963–1979: Conciliar, Papal and Curial Texts* (DOL) (Collegeville, Minn.: The Liturgical Press, 1982).

AP	Congregation for Divine Worship, instruction *Actio pastoralis.* (DOL 275)
CDW	Congregation for Divine Worship
CSL	*Constitution on the Sacred Liturgy (Sacrosanctum Concilium)*, Vatican Council II. (DOL 1)
DMC	*Directory for Masses with Children.* (DOL 276)
EM	Congregation of Rites, *Eucharisticum mysterium* (on Worship of the Eucharistic). (DOL 179)
GCD	*General Catechetical Directory*
GI	*General Instruction of the Roman Missal.* (DOL 208)
MS	Congregation of Rites, instruction *Musicam sacram.* (DOL 440)
RM	Roman Missal *(Missale Romanum)*

More Liturgical Resources

MEANINGFUL FIRST COMMUNION LITURGIES
The Complete Planning Guide
for Catechists and Teachers

Nick Wagner

Paper
128 pages, 8.5" x 11", 0-89390-432-5

This guide, designed to accompany any First Communion prepartation program, guides you toward First Communion liturgies that are truly prayerful. Too often First Communion liturgies are planned as crowd-pleasing spectacles. This guide shows you how to plan a liturgy that is respectful while giving full attention to the three primary principles of good liturgy. This guide is not meant to replace what you're currently doing, but to supplement your current program and help it evolve. Meaningful First Communions are not just about preparing the liturgy; they're also about preparing the assembly, the families and the children for the liturgy. That's why this guide includes photocopiable preparation notes to handout to all the participants of this important ritual. You'll learn everything you need to know, from the opening procession to the recessional song.

MODERN LITURGY ANSWERS
THE 101 MOST-ASKED QUESTIONS ABOUT LITURGY

Nick Wagner

Paper
144 pages, 5.5" x 8.5", 0-89390-369-8

Everyone has a question about liturgy. Get answers from the editor of MINISTRY & LITURGY magazine (formerly MODERN LITURGY). You'll learn the historical and theological background of current liturgical practices — and you'll get practical solutions to vexing pastoral problems. Use this important reference book for your planning — or just to provide quick authoritative answers.

THE WORD AND EUCHARIST HANDBOOK

Lawrence J. Johnson

Paper
168 pages, 6" x 9", 0-89390-276-4

The Word and Eucharist Handbook is your complete reference guide to liturgy. Designed for worship planners, ministers, and liturgical artists, it answers your questions about the origin, development, and modern practice of each part of the Mass.

THE LITURGICAL MUSIC ANSWER BOOK
ML Answers the 101 Most-Asked Questions

Peggy Lovrien

Paper
160 pages, 5.5" x 8.5", 0-89390-454-6
June 1999

Here is a virtual training manual for music directors, song leaders, and choir members. The Liturgical Music Answer Book helps parish liturgical music committees study the liturgical music documents of the church, discover the appropriate ways to choose music for the liturgy, and operate with confidence in their ministry as liturgical musicians. The convenient question and answer format makes this material quickly accessible to busy liturgical musicians. From the basic, "Why do we sing at Mass?" to the practical, "What is the best way to introduce a new song?" to the specific, "Why are seat cushions bad for liturgical music?" — music committees will find satisfying answers to their nagging liturgical music questions.

Free trial subscription to the new
MINISTRY & LITURGY magazine

Editor Nick Wagner

Ten issues per year.

If liturgy is the source and summit of parish life, it's your business — whether you are a liturgist, a religious educator, a youth minister, or a pastoral-care coordinator. That's why MODERN LITURGY (ML) has changed its name to MINISTRY & LITURGY. Check out the "new ML" for yourself. Just call us or visit our web site. You will receive the next issue of ML followed by an invoice. If you like what you see, return the invoice with a check to cover the subscription and receive the next nine issues. If you choose not to subscribe, just mark cancel on the invoice and return it. The first issue is yours to keep FREE.
Current ML subscribers: Pass on your copy of ML to a friend. Send us a copy of your ML mailing label and we'll send you a FREE replacement copy. Subscribe to ML today!

Order these books from your local bookseller or call:
1-888-273-7782 (toll free) or 1-408-286-8505
or visit the web site at www.rpinet.com

LITURGICAL MINISTRY
A Practical Guide to Spirituality

Donna Cole

Paper, (bulk prices available)
64 pages, 5.5" x 8.5", 0-89390-372-8

Support and affirm your volunteer liturgical ministers with this concise and practical book on spirituality. Working under the assumption that all liturgical ministry is important and should be prepared for prayerfully, Donna Cole uses the commissioning rite as the basis for the liturgical minister's formation. Front chapters on prayer and spirituality apply to all ministers. Back chapters provide practical tips specific to lectors, ministers of communion, musicians, ministers of hospitality, and servers.
"The material in this book will be helpful to those who serve as liturgical ministers whether they are just beginning or whether they have served for some time and are looking for something to renew themselves. Reading this book should help all ministers realize how important their ministry is."— National Bulletin on Liturgy

BUILDING SELF-ESTEEM
A Workbook for Teens

Jerome Trahey

Illustrated, Paper
128 pages, 8.5" x 11", 0-89390-231-4

This workbook gives teens practical, original exercises that can help them find out who they are, what they value, and where they are going with what they value. It uniquely helps them discover their innate goodness and worth in light of the Gospel. Bulk discounts available.

WHAT TO DO WHEN YOUR STUDENTS TALK DIRTY

Timothy Jay, PhD

Paper
160 pages, 5.5" x 8.5", 0-89390-363-9

Abusive language creates all kinds of legal, social, and interpersonal problems in schools. Finally you can do something about bad language on your campus. What to Do When Your Students Talk Dirty promotes teacher awareness of abusive language and shows them how to reduce the problem on campus. It stresses cognitive-
behavior strategies and practical ways of reducing bad language.

JOURNAL ME!
A Pocketbook for Girls

Helen Raica-Klotz

Paper
96 pages, 4.25" x 7", 0-89390-449-X
April 1999

Journal Me! A Pocketbook for Girls is a short, easy-to-read guide that girls can use to explore their individuality, identify self-defeating behavior patterns, take responsibility for their feelings and actions, make better choices, and achieve happiness. The pocketbook includes simple, fun exercises and space for recording ideas, reactions, and notes. It can be used independently or as a supporting resource for Empower Me! sessions.

EMPOWER ME!
12 Sessions for Building Self-Esteem in Girls

Helen Raica-Klotz

Paper
128 pages, 8.5" x 11", 0-89390-448-1
April 1999

While adult women have made great strides in the past 35 years, teenage girls seem to be backsliding. They are more likely than a boy to take up smoking, to try drugs, and to get a sexually transmitted disease. Empower Me! 12 Sessions for Building Self-Esteem in Girls is a manual that facilitators can use to run a self-esteem group for girls. The sessions help girls explore their individuality and improve relationships with family and friends. Because of the powerful nature of the Empower Me! exercises, facilitators should either be professional counselors themselves or collaborate with one.

THE YOUNG SERVER'S BOOK OF THE MASS

Kenneth Guentert

Paper (bulk prices available)
73 pages, 4" x 6", 0-89390-078-8

Here is the history of the Mass in the language of young people. With this background, servers can understand why they do what they do. You'll be pleased with the results: they'll feel and act like a special part of the liturgy.